Circle of Grace

CIRCLE
of GRACE

A Book *of* Blessings
for the Seasons

JAN RICHARDSON

Wanton Gospeller Press
ORLANDO, FLORIDA

janrichardson.com   wantongospeller.com

For Gary Doles

Most beloved blessing

Contents

THEREFORE I WILL HOPE
Holy Week & Easter

WHEN WE BREATHE TOGETHER
Ascension & Pentecost

WHERE THE HANDS MEET
Ordinary Time

Acknowledgments

I am grateful for the extraordinary circle of grace that has encompassed me as I have worked on this book. For particular graces that have made a difference in the book and in the writer, I thank Peg Carlson-Hoffman and Chuck Hoffman, Mary Stamps, Brenda Lewis, Karen Weatherford, Maru Ladròn de Guevara, Janice Elsheimer, the Richardson and Doles families, and everyone at Infusion Tea in College Park.

I am grateful to Jenee Woodard at The Text This Week (textweek.com) for her longtime support as I have created these blessings from season to season.

I owe particular gratitude to my friend and editor Christianne Squires, who blesses me in both these roles with remarkable grace, insight, and heart.

My husband, the singer/songwriter Garrison Doles, died suddenly before this book's completion. He had seen nearly every blessing first, and we had dreamed of this book together. His spirit infuses each page.

And to you, deep gratitude and every blessing.

Introduction

How did you become a writer of blessings? a friend recently asked.

The truth is, the blessings snuck up on me.

Blessings had visited from time to time, stealing their way into my work. The brief blessings I wrote to close each reading in my previous book, *In the Sanctuary of Women*, gave way to a longer blessing I composed for the day of my wedding five years ago. Soon after, I began writing blessings regularly for my blog *The Painted Prayerbook*, where I composed them in connection with the lectionary—the cycle of readings that carry us through much of the Bible.

One of the first readings to come around as I began writing blessings was the story of the raising of Lazarus in John 11. As I lived with this text in which Christ calls his friend to return across the threshold from death into life, it came home to me that the most profound blessings we will ever know are those that meet us in the place of our deepest loss and inspire us to choose to live again.

The secret of this blessing, I began to write as I reflected on the Lazarus text, *is that it is written on the back of what binds you.*

I found myself enchanted and compelled by the power of a blessing: how, in the space of a few lines, the stuff of pain, grief, and death becomes the very substance of hope. I wanted not only to know more about that place; I wanted to live there.

POETRY AND MYSTERY

An ancient literary form, a blessing is a distinctive constellation of words designed to call upon and convey God's deepest desire for our wholeness and well-being, both individually and in community. From Genesis through Revelation and throughout the Judeo-Christian tradition, some of the most powerful and beautiful texts are those of blessings.

Woven into the formality of liturgy as well as the workings of daily life, blessings are spoken upon all manner of people, activities, and objects. In their ubiquity and compelling variety, blessings illuminate the link between the sacred and the ordinary. They do more than simply call us to recognize the essential connection between these two realms of life; blessings enable us to perceive the ways the sacred inhabits the ordinary, impressing upon us that every moment and each place lies within the circle of God's care.

Blessings are often poetic, pulsing with the rhythms of invocation and incantation and taking on the cadence of litany and liturgy. They use ordinary language in ways that can become extraordinary, offering words that arrest our attention and awaken us to how the holy is at work in our very midst.

Yet for all its poetry and power, there is nothing inherently magical about a blessing. A blessing will not fix us. It will not, of itself, resolve the difficulty we are in or undo harm we have caused or received. Instead, a blessing is a channel of the Divine, a profound means of grace that has the capacity to open our eyes so that we might recognize and receive the help of the One who created us in love and whose deepest desire for us is that we be whole.

Although a blessing might not be magical, a good blessing nonetheless shimmers with the mystery that lies at the heart of God. A blessing speaks from God's mysterious heart into our own heart, meeting us in our ache for connection and presence. A blessing taps into our longing for what lies beyond our experience and understanding, helping us recognize how mystery makes its home within the familiar contours of our life.

We see this with such clarity in Celtic blessings, with their lines that call upon the divine presence that is ancient and otherworldly yet permeates all of creation here and now. With both poetry and mystery, these blessings encompass the most basic concerns of daily life: shelter, work, community, passages from birth through death—the places where God meets us and seeks to sustain us with the provision we most need.

The fact that blessings are so rooted in mystery means they rarely behave as we think they should. We often talk about blessings, in their more metaphorical sense, as though they are a reward or a sign of special status, a measure of God's providence toward us. Much of Christian culture equates blessings with prosperity, health, and abundance. While it is tempting to correlate such gifts with the favor of God, this notion holds an insidious corollary: that those who are not prosperous, those who are sick, those whom misfortune has visited—these have not received the blessing of God.

In fact, blessings often work in quite the contrary kind of way. Rather than being an indicator or measure of God's favor, a true blessing most often meets us in the place of our greatest need, desperation, pain, or lack. By design, a blessing finds us when it has become difficult to perceive the providence of God—those occasions when the benevolence of God is hard to fathom.

To Invoke and Provoke

A blessing typically has a quality of invocation. It calls upon the presence of God and asks for the aid of the Divine, often in times of peril or pain. As part of our asking, a blessing invites us to open our hands to receive what God offers in response—to turn ourselves toward the blessing God most wants to give to us. It is no small thing to allow ourselves to receive this gift, this blessing, especially when it comes in a form we did not expect and perhaps would not have chosen for ourselves.

Yet a true blessing does more than invoke the presence and response of God; it is meant also to provoke us, to incite *us* to a response. The best blessings awaken our imaginations. In places of difficulty, struggle, or pain, blessings beckon us to look closely rather than turn away. In such places, they challenge us not to accept how things are but to dream of how they could be transformed. They invite us to discern how God might be calling us to participate in bringing this transformation to pass.

The story of Mary's visit to Elizabeth in the gospel of Luke illuminates this capacity a blessing holds to not only perceive what is, but also imagine what could be. Finding herself pregnant, unmarried, and quite alone following the archangel Gabriel's astonishing visit, during which she offered her radical consent to become the mother of Christ, Mary flees to the home of her kinswoman Elizabeth. There she finds a place of sanctuary, solace, and blessing. *Blessed are you among women*, Elizabeth cries out when Mary enters her home, *and blessed is the fruit of your womb*.

Mary basks in Elizabeth's blessing, but she does not stop there. She responds with the song we have come to know as the Magnificat, a stunning poem of praise to the God who redeems and restores the world.

Mary and Elizabeth's story provides a model of what a blessing can do. In their encounter, we witness the power of a blessing to encompass us with shelter and sanctuary even as it frees us to imagine and live into a world made new.

THE SACRED YEAR

Some of the most beautiful and powerful blessings of the Christian tradition are those connected with the seasons and the turning of time, which is, in itself, a place of deep mystery. These blessings show us that within the rhythms of *chronos* time—the Greek term for linear, chronological time—there exists the dance of time known as *kairos*. *Kairos* is the fullness of time, the appointed time, time beyond time.

Such blessings help open our eyes to *kairos* time and draw us into what Celtic folk have long called a *thin place*—a space where the veil between worlds becomes permeable, and heaven and earth meet. Thin places assure us that what we can see is not all there is, that within the struggle, joy, pain, and delight that attend our life, there is an invisible circle of grace that enfolds and encompasses us in every moment. Blessings help us to perceive this circle of grace, to find our place of belonging within it, and to receive the strength the circle holds for us.

In the Christian tradition, the sacred year is itself a circle that draws us into the ongoing story of God with us. Season by season, the Christian year invites us to travel through the stories, traditions, rituals, and memories that help us know who we are as the people of God. Living in concert with the turning of the sacred year helps us enter into time with intention and mindfulness, rather than letting events propel us along.

The blessings within this book, which will be the first in a series of books of blessings, arose from my journey with the seasons. I wrote most of them for my blogs *The Painted Prayerbook* and *The Advent Door* as I engaged the readings that accompany us through Advent and Christmas, Epiphany, Transfiguration Day, Lent, Holy Week and Easter, Ascension Day and Pentecost, and the beginning of Ordinary Time.

In the Epiphany section, you will find blessings for the holiday known as Women's Christmas. Originating in Ireland, where it is known as *Nollaig na mBan*, Women's Christmas began as a day when the women, who often carried the domestic responsibilities all year, took Epiphany Day (January 6) as an occasion to enjoy a break and celebrate together at the end of the holidays. Such a day reminds us that rest is a crucial element in the rhythm of the sacred year.

As we journey again and again through each season, our path is never precisely the same. The seasons change us. With each one, we move ever further into the circle that encompasses us and into the grace we find there. Circle becomes spiral, bearing us deeper and deeper into the heart of God.

The Blessing We Most Need

In the end, I am not entirely certain why I became a writer of blessings. I have a penchant for poetry and mystery and so am compelled to explore how they work together within the space of a blessing. I have come to suspect, however, that one of the primary reasons I began to compose blessings is because I am in such need of them myself.

I learned this most especially after the unexpected death of my husband nearly two years ago. An astounding source of blessing and grace in my life, Gary died at the beginning of Advent, several weeks after experiencing complications during what we had anticipated would be routine surgery. We had been married less than four years. Even now I find it both eerie and beautiful to come across a blessing that I wrote before he died (such as "A Blessing to Summon Rejoicing," included here in the Advent section) and realize it is one that I so need.

Such moments serve to show that blessings do not typically work in a linear way. They twist and turn, make their own paths, and spiral back to find us when we most need to receive them. Healing the fractured past, provoking us to act for a more whole future, opening our eyes to the God who meets us in the present—blessings work within time but are not bound by it. They are the stuff of poetry and mystery, of *kairos* and thin places, made of the most ordinary of moments yet holding the power to open us to eternity.

A blessing is, finally, something wild. It leads us where we did not imagine to go, and never in a straight line. That is the nature of a blessing—and the nature of God, who meets us in each moment, within time and beyond it, encompassing us season by season in a circle of grace.

Jan Richardson
Feast of All Saints 2015

Where the Light Begins

---

*Blessings for
Advent & Christmas*

*"And what I say to you
I say to all: Keep awake."*
—MARK 13:37

BLESSING FOR WAKING

This blessing could
pound on your door
in the middle of
the night.

This blessing could
bang on your window,
could tap dance
in your hall,
could set a dog loose
in your room.

It could hire a
brass band
to play outside
your house.

But what this blessing
really wants
is not merely
your waking
but your company.

This blessing
wants to sit
alongside you
and keep vigil
with you.
This blessing
wishes to wait
with you.

And so,
though it is capable
of causing a cacophony
that could raise
the dead,

this blessing
will simply
lean toward you
and sing quietly
in your ear
a song to lull you
not into sleep
but into waking.

It will tell you stories
that hold you breathless
till the end.

It will ask you questions
you never considered
and have you tell it

what you saw
in your dreaming.

This blessing
will do all within
its power
to entice you
into awareness

because it wants
to be there,
to bear witness,
to see the look
in your eyes
on the day when
your vigil is complete
and all your waiting
has come to
its joyous end.

No eye has seen any God besides you,
who works for those who wait for him.
—ISAIAH 64:4

BLESSING THE DOOR

First let us say
a blessing
upon all who have
entered here before
us.

You can see the sign
of their passage
by the worn place
where their hand rested
on the doorframe
as they walked through,
the smooth sill
of the threshold
where they crossed.

Press your ear
to the door
for a moment before
you enter,

and you will hear
their voices murmuring

words you cannot
quite make out
but know
are full of welcome.

On the other side,
these ones who wait—
for you,
if you do not
know by now—
understand what
a blessing can do:

how it appears like
nothing you expected;

how it arrives as
visitor,
outrageous invitation,
child;

how it takes the form
of angel
or dream;

how it comes
in words like
How can this be?
and
lifted up the lowly;

how it sounds like
in the wilderness
prepare the way.

Those who wait
for you know
how the mark of
a true blessing
is that it will take you
where you did not
think to go.

Once through this door,
there will be more:
more doors,
more blessings,
more who watch and
wait for you.

But here
at this door of
beginning,
the blessing cannot
be said without you.

So lay your palm
against the frame
that those before you
touched.

Place your feet
where others paused
in this entryway.

Say the thing that
you most need,
and the door will
open wide.

And by this word
the door is blessed,
and by this word
the blessing is begun
from which,
door by door,
all the rest
will come.

Make me to know your ways, O LORD;
teach me your paths.
—PSALM 25:4

A BLESSING FOR TRAVELING IN THE DARK

Go slow
if you can.
Slower.
More slowly still.
Friendly dark
or fearsome,
this is no place
to break your neck
by rushing,
by running,
by crashing into
what you cannot see.

Then again,
it is true:
different darks
have different tasks,
and if you
have arrived here unawares,
if you have come
in peril
or in pain,

this might be no place
you should dawdle.

I do not know
what these shadows
ask of you,
what they might hold
that means you good
or ill.
It is not for me
to reckon
whether you should linger
or you should leave.

But this is what
I can ask for you:

That in the darkness
there be a blessing.
That in the shadows
there be a welcome.
That in the night
you be encompassed
by the Love that knows
your name.

*"Now when these things begin
to take place, stand up and
raise your heads, because your
redemption is drawing near."*
—LUKE 21:28

DRAWING NEAR

It is difficult to see it from here,
I know,
but trust me when I say
this blessing is inscribed
on the horizon.
Is written on
that far point
you can hardly see.
Is etched into
a landscape
whose contours you cannot know
from here.
All you know
is that it calls you,
draws you,
pulls you toward
what you have perceived
only in pieces,
in fragments that came to you
in dreaming
or in prayer.

I cannot account for how,
as you draw near,
the blessing embedded in the horizon
begins to blossom
upon the soles of your feet,
shimmers in your two hands.
It is one of the mysteries
of the road,
how the blessing
you have traveled toward,
waited for,
ached for
suddenly appears,
as if it had been with you
all this time,
as if it simply
needed to know
how far you were willing
to walk
to find the lines
that were traced upon you
before the day
you were born.

"The sun will be darkened...
and the powers in the heavens
will be shaken."
—MARK 13:24–25

BLESSING WHEN THE WORLD IS ENDING

Look, the world
is always ending
somewhere.

Somewhere
the sun has come
crashing down.

Somewhere
it has gone
completely dark.

Somewhere
it has ended
with the gun,
the knife,
the fist.

Somewhere
it has ended
with the slammed door,
the shattered hope.

Somewhere
it has ended
with the utter quiet
that follows the news
from the phone,
the television,
the hospital room.

Somewhere
it has ended
with a tenderness
that will break
your heart.

But, listen,
this blessing means
to be anything
but morose.
It has not come
to cause despair.

It is here
simply because
there is nothing
a blessing
is better suited for
than an ending,
nothing that cries out more
for a blessing
than when a world
is falling apart.

This blessing
will not fix you,
will not mend you,
will not give you
false comfort;
it will not talk to you
about one door opening
when another one closes.

It will simply
sit itself beside you
among the shards
and gently turn your face
toward the direction
from which the light
will come,
gathering itself
about you
as the world begins
again.

*"See, I am sending my
messenger ahead of you,
who will prepare your way."*
—MARK 1:2

BLESSING THE WAY

With every step
you take,
this blessing rises up
to meet you.

It has been waiting
long ages for you.

Look close
and you can see
the layers of it,

how it has been fashioned
by those who walked
this road before you,

how it has been created
of nothing but
their determination
and their dreaming,

how it has taken
its form

from an ancient hope
that drew them forward
and made a way for them
when no way could be
seen.

Look closer
and you will see
this blessing
is not finished,

that you are part
of the path
it is preparing,

that you are how
this blessing means
to be a voice
within the wilderness

and a welcome
for the way.

We wait for new heavens
and a new earth.
—2 PETER 3:13

BLESSING FOR WAITING

Who wait
for the night
to end

bless them.

Who wait
for the night
to begin

bless them.

Who wait
in the hospital room
who wait
in the cell
who wait
in prayer

bless them.

Who wait
for news

who wait
for the phone call
who wait
for a word

who wait
for a job
a house
a child

bless them.

Who wait
for one who
will come home

who wait
for one who
will not come home

bless them.

Who wait with fear
who wait with joy
who wait with peace
who wait with rage

who wait for the end
who wait for the beginning
who wait alone
who wait together

bless them.

Who wait
without knowing
what they wait for
or why

bless them.

Who wait
when they
should not wait
who wait
when they should be
in motion
who wait
when they need
to rise
who wait
when they need
to set out

bless them.

Who wait
for the end
of waiting
who wait
for the fullness
of time
who wait
emptied and
open and
ready

who wait
for you,

O bless.

"Prepare the way of the Lord,
make his paths straight."
—LUKE 3:4

PREPARE

Strange how one word
will so hollow you out.
But this word
has been in the wilderness
for months.
Years.

This word is what remained
after everything else
was worn away
by sand and stone.
It is what withstood
the glaring of sun by day,
the weeping loneliness of
the moon at night.

Now it comes to you
racing out of the wild,
eyes blazing
and waving its arms,
its voice ragged with desert
but piercing and loud

as it speaks itself
again and again:

Prepare, prepare.

It may feel like
the word is leveling you,
emptying you
as it asks you
to give up
what you have known.

It is impolite
and hardly tame,
but when it falls
upon your lips
you will wonder
at the sweetness,

like honey
that finds its way
into the hunger
you had not known
was there.

May those who sow in tears
reap with shouts of joy.
—PSALM 126:5

BLESSING TO SUMMON REJOICING

When your weeping
has watered
the earth.

When the storm
has been long
and the night
and the season
of your sorrowing.

When you have seemed
an exile
from your life,
lost in the far country,
a long way from where
your comfort lies.

When the sound
of splintering
and fracture
haunts you.

When despair
attends you.

When lack.
When trouble.
When fear.
When pain.

When empty.
When lonely.
When too much
of what depletes you
and not enough
of what restores
and rests you.

Then let there be
rejoicing.

Then let there be
dreaming.

Let there be
laughter in your mouth
and on your tongue
shouts of joy.

Let the seeds
soaked by tears
turn to grain,
to bread,
to feasting.

Let there be
coming home.

He came as a witness
to testify to the light.
—JOHN 1:7

BLESSED ARE YOU WHO BEAR THE LIGHT

Blessed are you
who bear the light
in unbearable times,
who testify
to its endurance
amid the unendurable,
who bear witness
to its persistence
when everything seems
in shadow
and grief.

Blessed are you
in whom
the light lives,
in whom
the brightness blazes—
your heart
a chapel,
an altar where
in the deepest night
can be seen
the fire that

shines forth in you
in unaccountable faith,
in stubborn hope,
in love that illumines
every broken thing
it finds.

*He will rejoice over you with gladness,
he will renew you in his love;
he will exult over you with loud singing
as on a day of festival.*
—ZEPHANIAH 3:17–18

AS ON A DAY OF FESTIVAL

Call it
the waters of salvation
or the garlands of gladness.

Call it
the grave-clothes
falling away,
or call it the loosing
of the chains.

Call it
what binds us together:
fierce but
fragile but
fierce.

Call it
*he will rejoice over you
with gladness*;
call it
*he will renew you
in his love*;

call it
he will exult over you
with loud singing
as on a day
of festival.

Call it
the thin, thin place
where the veil
gives way.

Or call it this:
the path we make
when we go deep
and deeper still
into the dark
and look behind to see
the way has been lit
by our rejoicing.

A BLESSING FOR AFTER

This blessing
is for the moment
after clarity has come,
after inspiration,
after you have agreed
to what seems
impossible.

This blessing
is what follows
after illumination departs
and you realize
there is no map
for the path
you have chosen,
no one to serve
as guide,
nothing to do
but gather up
your gumption
and set out.

This blessing
will go with you.
It carries no answers,
no charts,
no plans.

It carries no source
of light
within itself.

But in its pocket
is tucked a mirror
that, from time to time,
it will hold up to you

to remind you
of the radiance
that came
when you gave
your awful and wondrous
yes.

ELIZABETH'S BLESSING

On the day
when you have agreed
to what you could never
have imagined,
let this blessing
first lay its hands
upon your belly,
your brow.

Let this blessing draw you
into the litany
of your breathing in,
your breathing out—
the ceremony of
the beating of
your heart
as it spends itself
in gathering
and release.

Look at each thing
you have drawn into
the circle of your life:

fashioned of
glass and stone,
paper and clay;
how each object
remains unchanged
but for how
it now inhabits this world
where you have
spoken *yes*,
have offered the word
you will never now
unsay.

She entered the house of Zechariah
and greeted Elizabeth.
—LUKE 1:40

A BLESSING CALLED SANCTUARY

You hardly knew
how hungry you were
to be gathered in,
to receive the welcome
that invited you to enter
entirely—
nothing of you
found foreign or strange,
nothing of your life
that you were asked
to leave behind
or to carry in silence
or in shame.

Tentative steps
became settling in,
leaning into the blessing
that enfolded you,
taking your place
in the circle
that stunned you
with its unimagined grace.

You began to breathe again,
to move without fear,
to speak with abandon
the words you carried
in your bones,
that echoed in your being.

You learned to sing.

But the deal with this blessing
is that it will not leave you alone,
will not let you linger
in safety,
in stasis.

The time will come
when this blessing
will ask you to leave,
not because it has tired of you
but because it desires for you
to become the sanctuary
that you have found—
to speak your word
into the world,
to tell what you have heard
with your own ears,
seen with your own eyes,
known in your own heart:

that you are beloved,
precious child of God,
beautiful to behold,*

and you are welcome
and more than welcome
here.

---

*Thanks to the Rev. Janet Wolf and the congregation of Hobson United Methodist Church in Nashville, Tennessee, for the story in which these words—"beloved, precious child of God, and beautiful to behold"—were offered to help transform the life of a member of their community. The story appears in The Upper Room Disciplines 1999 (Nashville: The Upper Room).

FOR JOY

You can prepare,
but still
it will come to you
by surprise,

crossing through your doorway,
calling your name in greeting,
turning like a child
who quickens suddenly
within you.

It will astonish you
how wide your heart
will open
in welcome

for the joy
that finds you
so ready
and still so
unprepared.

The people who walked in darkness
have seen a great light; those who
lived in a land of deep darkness—
on them light has shined.
—Isaiah 9:2

How the Light Comes
For Christmas Eve

I cannot tell you
how the light comes.

What I know
is that it is more ancient
than imagining.

That it travels
across an astounding expanse
to reach us.

That it loves
searching out
what is hidden,
what is lost,
what is forgotten
or in peril
or in pain.

That it has a fondness
for the body,
for finding its way

toward flesh,
for tracing the edges
of form,
for shining forth
through the eye,
the hand,
the heart.

I cannot tell you
how the light comes,
but that it does.
That it will.
That it works its way
into the deepest dark
that enfolds you,
though it may seem
long ages in coming
or arrive in a shape
you did not foresee.

And so
may we this day
turn ourselves toward it.
May we lift our faces
to let it find us.
May we bend our bodies
to follow the arc it makes.
May we open
and open more
and open still
to the blessed light
that comes.

The light shines in the darkness,
and the darkness did not overcome it.
—JOHN 1:5

WHERE THE LIGHT BEGINS
For Christmas Day

Perhaps it does not begin.
Perhaps it is always.

Perhaps it takes
a lifetime
to open our eyes,
to learn to see
what has forever
shimmered in front of us—

the luminous line
of the map
in the dark,

the vigil flame
in the house
of the heart,

the love
so searing
we cannot keep
from singing,

from crying out
in testimony
and praise.

Perhaps this day
will be the mountain
over which
the dawn breaks.

Perhaps we
will turn our face
toward it,
toward what has been
always.

Perhaps
our eyes
will finally open
in ancient recognition,
willingly dazzled,
illuminated at last.

Perhaps this day
the light begins
in us.

For Those Who Have Far to Travel

Blessings for
Epiphany & Women's Christmas

*"We observed his star at its rising,
and have come to pay him homage."*
—MATTHEW 2:2

WHERE THE MAP BEGINS

This is not
any map you know.
Forget longitude.
Forget latitude.
Do not think
of distances
or of plotting
the most direct route.
Astrolabe, sextant, compass:
these will not help you here.

This is the map
that begins with a star.
This is the chart
that starts with fire,
with blazing,
with an ancient light
that has outlasted
generations, empires,
cultures, wars.

Look starward once,
then look away.

Close your eyes
and see how the map
begins to blossom
behind your lids,
how it constellates,
its lines stretching out
from where you stand.

You cannot see it all,
cannot divine the way
it will turn and spiral,
cannot perceive how
the road you walk
will lead you finally inside,
through the labyrinth
of your own heart
and belly
and lungs.

But step out
and you will know
what the wise who traveled
this path before you
knew:
the treasure in this map
is buried
not at journey's end
but at its beginning.

And there, ahead of them,
went the star that they
had seen at its rising.
—Matthew 2:9

For Those Who Have Far to Travel

If you could see
the journey whole,
you might never
undertake it,
might never dare
the first step
that propels you
from the place
you have known
toward the place
you know not.

Call it
one of the mercies
of the road:
that we see it
only by stages
as it opens
before us,
as it comes into
our keeping,
step by
single step.

There is nothing
for it
but to go,
and by our going
take the vows
the pilgrim takes:

to be faithful to
the next step;
to rely on more
than the map;
to heed the signposts
of intuition and dream;
to follow the star
that only you
will recognize;

to keep an open eye
for the wonders that
attend the path;
to press on
beyond distractions,
beyond fatigue,
beyond what would
tempt you
from the way.

There are vows
that only you
will know:
the secret promises
for your particular path

and the new ones
you will need to make
when the road
is revealed
by turns
you could not
have foreseen.

Keep them, break them,
make them again;
each promise becomes
part of the path,
each choice creates
the road
that will take you
to the place
where at last
you will kneel

to offer the gift
most needed—
the gift that only you
can give—
before turning to go
home by
another way.

And having been warned in a dream
not to return to Herod, they left for
their own country by another road.
—MATTHEW 2:12

BLESSING OF THE MAGI

There is no reversing
this road.
The path that bore you here
goes in one direction only,
every step drawing you
down a way
by which you will not
return.

You thought arrival
was everything,
that your entire journey
ended with kneeling
in the place
you had spent all
to find.

When you laid down
your gift,
release came with such ease,
your treasure tumbling
from your hands

in awe and
benediction.

Now the knowledge
of your leaving
comes like a stone laid
over your heart,
the familiar path closed
and not even the solace
of a star
to guide your way.

You will set out in fear.
You will set out in dream.

But you will set out

by that other road
that lies in shadow
and in dark.

We cannot show you
what route will
take you home;
that way is yours
and will be found
in the walking.

But we tell you,
you will wonder
at how the light you thought
you had left behind

goes with you,
spilling from
your empty hands,
shimmering beneath
your homeward feet,
illuminating the road
with every step
you take.

Arise, shine;
for your light has come.
—Isaiah 60:1

The Shimmering Hours
For Women's Christmas

There is so much
I want to say,
as if the saying
could prepare you
for this path,
as if there were anything
I could offer
that would make your way
less circuitous,
more smooth.

Once you step out,
you will see for yourself
how nothing could have
made you ready for this road
that will take you
from what you know
to what you cannot perceive
except, perhaps,
in your dreaming
or as it gives a glimpse
in prayer.

But I can tell you
this journey is not
about miles.
It is not about how far
you can walk
or how fast.

It is about what you will do
with this moment, this star
that blazes in your sky
though no one else
might see.

So open your heart
to these shimmering hours
by which your path
is made.

Open your eyes
to the light that shines
on what you will need
to see.

Open your hands
to those who go with you,
those seen
and those known only
by their blessing,
their benediction
of the road that is
your own.

Lift up your eyes and look around;
they all gather together, they come to you.
—Isaiah 60:4

I Know How Far
For Women's Christmas

I know how far
you would walk
to offer what
is needed,
the lengths
you would go to
to provide for those
you hold dear.

I know how every road
you travel
begins in the hollow
of your chest,
in the chambers
of your heart;
how you measure
your steps
by the rhythm
of your pulse;
how you find
your way
across terrains

no map
could ever show.

No distance,
no barrier,
no expanse of time
would keep you
from propelling yourself
toward the place where
your heart has already
arrived.

But for a moment,
for one small space
of time,
could you pause
and in the quiet
wait
for the gifts
that have been gathering
around you,
the treasures borne
by those
who have been traveling
to welcome you
since the moment
you left home?

"Bring my sons from far away and
my daughters from the end of the earth."
—Isaiah 43:6

The Map You Make Yourself
For Women's Christmas

You have looked
at so many doors
with longing,
wondering if your life
lay on the other side.

For today,
choose the door
that opens
to the inside.

Travel the most ancient way
of all:
the path that leads you
to the center
of your life.

No map
but the one
you make yourself.

No provision
but what you already carry
and the grace that comes
to those who walk
the pilgrim's way.

Speak this blessing
as you set out
and watch how
your rhythm slows,
the cadence of the road
drawing you into the pace
that is your own.

Eat when hungry.
Rest when tired.
Listen to your dreaming.
Welcome detours
as doors deeper in.

Pray for protection.
Ask for guidance.
Offer gladness
for the gifts that come,
and then
let them go.

Do not expect
to return
by the same road.
Home is always
by another way,

and you will know it
not by the light
that waits for you

but by the star
that blazes inside you,
telling you
where you are
is holy
and you are welcome
here.

When Glory

Blessings for
Transfiguration Day

*"Master, it is good for us to be here;
let us make three dwellings, one for you,
one for Moses, and one for Elijah."*
—LUKE 9:33

DAZZLING

Believe me, I know
how tempting it is
to remain inside this blessing,
to linger where everything
is dazzling
and clear.

We could build walls
around this blessing,
put a roof over it.
We could bring in
a table, chairs,
have the most amazing meals.
We could make a home.
We could stay.

But this blessing
is built for leaving.
This blessing
is made for coming down
the mountain.
This blessing
wants to be in motion,

to travel with you
as you return
to level ground.

It will seem strange
how quiet this blessing becomes
when it returns to earth.
It is not shy.
It is not afraid.

It simply knows
how to bide its time,
to watch and wait,
to discern and pray

until the moment comes
when it will reveal
everything it knows,
when it will shine forth
with all it has seen,
when it will dazzle
with the unforgettable light
you have carried
all this way.

Since they had stayed awake,
they saw his glory and the two
men who stood with him.
—LUKE 9:32

WHEN GLORY

That when glory comes,
we will open our eyes
to see it.

That when glory shows up,
we will let ourselves
be overcome
not by fear
but by the love
it bears.

That when glory shines,
we will bring it
back with us
all the way,
all the way,
all the way down.

Beloved Is Where We Begin

Blessings for Lent

BLESSING THE DUST
For Ash Wednesday

All those days
you felt like dust,
like dirt,
as if all you had to do
was turn your face
toward the wind
and be scattered
to the four corners

or swept away
by the smallest breath
as insubstantial—

did you not know
what the Holy One
can do with dust?

This is the day
we freely say
we are scorched.

This is the hour
we are marked

by what has made it
through the burning.

This is the moment
we ask for the blessing
that lives within
the ancient ashes,
that makes its home
inside the soil of
this sacred earth.

So let us be marked
not for sorrow.
And let us be marked
not for shame.
Let us be marked
not for false humility
or for thinking
we are less
than we are

but for claiming
what God can do
within the dust,
within the dirt,
within the stuff
of which the world
is made
and the stars that blaze
in our bones
and the galaxies that spiral
inside the smudge
we bear.

You shall call, and the LORD will answer;
you shall cry for help, and he will say,
Here I am.
—ISAIAH 58:9

WILL YOU MEET US?
For Ash Wednesday

Will you meet us
in the ashes,
will you meet us
in the ache
and show your face
within our sorrow
and offer us
your word of grace:

that you are life
within the dying,
that you abide
within the dust,
that you are what
survives the burning,
that you arise
to make us new.

And in our aching,
you are breathing;
and in our weeping,
you are here

within the hands
that bear your blessing,
enfolding us
within your love.

Even now, says the LORD, return to me
with all your heart, with fasting,
with weeping, and with mourning;
rend your hearts and not your clothing.
—JOEL 2:12–13

REND YOUR HEART
For Ash Wednesday

To receive this blessing,
all you have to do
is let your heart break.
Let it crack open.
Let it fall apart
so you can see
its secret chambers,
the hidden spaces
where you have hesitated
to go.

Your entire life
is here, inscribed whole
upon your heart's walls:
every path taken
or left behind,
every face you turned toward
or turned away,
every word spoken in love
or in rage,
every line of your life
you would prefer to leave

in shadow,
every story that shimmers
with treasures known
and those you have yet
to find.

It could take you days
to wander these rooms.
Forty, at least.

And so let this be
a season for wandering,
for trusting the breaking,
for tracing the rupture
that will return you

to the One who waits,
who watches,
who works within
the rending
to make your heart
whole.

Return to the LORD, your God,
for he is gracious and merciful,
slow to anger, and abounding
in steadfast love.
—JOEL 2:13

RETURN
For Ash Wednesday

Remember.
You were built for this,
the ancient path
inscribed upon your bones,
the persistent pattern
echoing in your heartbeat.

Let this be the season
you turn your face
toward the One
who calls to you:

Return, return.

Let this be the day
you open wide your arms
to the wind that knows
how to bear you
home.

And a voice from heaven said,
"This is my Son, the Beloved,
with whom I am well pleased."
—MATTHEW 3:17

BELOVED IS WHERE WE BEGIN

If you would enter
into the wilderness,
do not begin
without a blessing.

Do not leave
without hearing
who you are:
Beloved,
named by the One
who has traveled this path
before you.

Do not go
without letting it echo
in your ears,
and if you find
it is hard
to let it into your heart,
do not despair.
That is what
this journey is for.

I cannot promise
this blessing will free you
from danger,
from fear,
from hunger
or thirst,
from the scorching
of sun
or the fall
of the night.

But I can tell you
that on this path
there will be help.

I can tell you
that on this way
there will be rest.

I can tell you
that you will know
the strange graces
that come to our aid
only on a road
such as this,
that fly to meet us
bearing comfort
and strength,
that come alongside us
for no other cause
than to lean themselves
toward our ear

and with their
curious insistence
whisper our name:

Beloved.
Beloved.
Beloved.

Jesus was led up by the Spirit
into the wilderness.
—MATTHEW 4:1

WILDERNESS BLESSING

Let us say
this blessing began
whole and complete
upon the page.

And then let us say
one word loosed itself
and another followed it
in turn.

Let us say
this blessing started
to shed all
it did not need,

that line by line
it returned
to the ground
from which it came.

Let us say
this blessing is not
leaving you,

is not abandoning you
to the wild
that lies ahead,

but that it is loathe
to load you down
on this road where
you will need
to travel light.

Let us say
perhaps this blessing
became the path
beneath your feet,
the desert
that stretched before you,
the clear sight
that finally came.

Let us say
that when this blessing
at last came to its end,
all it left behind
was bread,
wine,
a fleeting flash
of wing.

He fasted forty days and forty nights.
—MATTHEW 4:2

WHERE THE BREATH BEGINS

Dry
and dry
and dry
in each direction.

Dust dry.
Desert dry.
Bone dry.

And here
in your own heart:
dry,
the center of your chest
a bare valley
stretching out
every way you turn.

Did you think
this was where
you had come to die?

It's true that
you may need

to do some crumbling,
yes.
That some things
you have protected
may want to be
laid bare,
yes.
That you will be asked
to let go
and let go,
yes.

But listen.
This is what
a desert is for.

If you have come here
desolate,
if you have come here
deflated,
then thank your lucky stars
the desert is where
you have landed—
here where it is hard
to hide,
here where it is unwise
to rely on your own devices,
here where you will
have to look
and look again
and look close

to find what refreshment waits
to reveal itself to you.

I tell you,
though it may be hard
to see it now,
this is where
your greatest blessing
will find you.

I tell you,
this is where
you will receive
your life again.

I tell you,
this is where
the breath begins.

And the angels waited on him.
—MARK 1:13

BLESSING THAT MEETS YOU IN THE WILDERNESS

After the
desert stillness.

After the
wrestling.

After the
hours
and days
and weeks
of emptying.

After the
hungering
and the
thirsting.

After the
opening
and seeing
and knowing.

Let this blessing be
the first sweetness
that touches
your lips,

the bread
that falls into
your arms,

the cup
that welcoming hands
press into
yours.

Let this blessing be
the road that
returns you.

Let it be
the strength to carry
the wilderness
home.

BLESSING IN THE ROUND

This blessing
cannot help it;
it's the way
it was designed.

Lay it down
and it rises again.

Release it
and it returns.

Give it away
and it makes a path
back to you.

There is no explaining
how it delights
in reappearing
when you have ceased
to hold it,
no hiding the sly smile
it wears
when it shows up

at your door,
no mistaking the wonder
when it circles back around
just at the moment
you thought you had
spent it completely,
had poured it out
with abandon
where you saw
the deepest thirst for it,
had put it entirely
in the hands
of those desperate
in their hunger.

But here it is,
the perfect circle of it
pressing into your hand
that curls around it
and then lets go,
receiving
and releasing
and receiving again,
like the breath
that does not belong to us
but sets us in motion.

Rough Translations

Hope nonetheless.
Hope despite.
Hope regardless.
Hope still.

Hope where we had ceased to hope.
Hope amid what threatens hope.
Hope with those who feed our hope.
Hope beyond what we had hoped.

Hope that draws us past our limits.
Hope that defies expectations.
Hope that questions what we have known.
Hope that makes a way where there is none.

Hope that takes us past our fear.
Hope that calls us into life.
Hope that holds us beyond death.
Hope that blesses those to come.

*A Samaritan woman came
to draw water, and Jesus said
to her, "Give me a drink."*
—JOHN 4:7

BLESSING OF THE WELL

If you stand
at the edge
of this blessing
and call down
into it,
you will hear
your words
return to you.

If you lean in
and listen close,
you will hear
this blessing
give the story
of your life
back to you.

Quiet your voice.
Quiet your judgment.
Quiet the way
you always tell
your story
to yourself.

Quiet all these
and you will hear
the whole of it
and the hollows of it:
the spaces
in the telling,
the gaps
where you hesitate
to go.

Sit at the rim
of this blessing.
Press your ear
to its lip,
its sides,
its curves
that were carved out
long ago
by those whose thirst
drove them deep,
those who dug
into the layers
with only their hands
and hope.

Rest yourself
beside this blessing
and you will
begin to hear
the sound of water
entering the gaps.

Still yourself
and you will feel it
rising up within you,
filling every emptiness,
springing forth
anew.

"This temple has been under construction for forty-six years, and will you raise it up in three days?" But he was speaking of the temple of his body.
—JOHN 2:20–21

BLESSING THE BODY

This blessing takes
one look at you
and all it can say is
holy.

Holy hands.
Holy face.
Holy feet.
Holy everything
in between.

Holy even in pain.
Holy even when weary.
In brokenness, holy.
In shame, holy still.

Holy in delight.
Holy in distress.
Holy when being born.
Holy when we lay it down
at the hour of our death.

So, friend,
open your eyes
(holy eyes).
For one moment
see what this blessing sees,
this blessing that knows
how you have been formed
and knit together
in wonder and
in love.

Welcome this blessing
that folds its hands
in prayer
when it meets you;
receive this blessing
that wants to kneel
in reverence
before you—
you who are
temple,
sanctuary,
home for God
in this world.

*"He put mud on my eyes.
Then I washed, and now I see."*
—John 9:15

Blessing of Mud

Lest we think
the blessing
is not
in the dirt.

Lest we think
the blessing
is not
in the earth
beneath our feet.

Lest we think
the blessing
is not
in the dust,

like the dust
that God scooped up
at the beginning
and formed
with God's
two hands
and breathed into

with God's own
breath.

Lest we think
the blessing
is not
in the spit.

Lest we think
the blessing
is not
in the mud.

Lest we think
the blessing
is not
in the mire,
the grime,
the muck.

Lest we think
God cannot reach
deep into the things
of earth,
cannot bring forth
the blessing
that shimmers
within the sludge,
cannot anoint us
with a tender
and grimy grace.

Lest we think
God will not use
the ground
to give us
life again,
to cleanse us
of our unseeing,
to open our eyes upon
this ordinary
and stunning world.

*"Unless a grain of wheat
falls into the earth and dies,
it remains just a single grain;
but if it dies, it bears much fruit."*
—JOHN 12:24

BLESSING THE SEED

I should tell you
at the outset:
this blessing will require you
to do some work.

First you must simply
let this blessing fall
from your hand,
as if it were a small thing
you could easily let slip
through your fingers,
as if it were not
most precious to you,
as if your life did not
depend on it.

Next you must trust
that this blessing knows
where it is going,
that it understands
the ways of the dark,
that it is wise

to seasons
and to times.

Then—
and I know this blessing
has already asked much
of you—
it is to be hoped that
you will rest
and learn
that something is at work
when all seems still,
seems dormant,
seems dead.

I promise you
this blessing has not
abandoned you.
I promise you
this blessing
is on its way back
to you.
I promise you—
when you are least
expecting it,
when you have given up
your last hope—
this blessing will rise
green
and whole
and new.

He cried with a loud voice,
"Lazarus, come out!"
—JOHN 11:43

LAZARUS BLESSING

The secret
of this blessing
is that it is written
on the back
of what binds you.

To read
this blessing,
you must take hold
of the end
of what
confines you,
must begin to tug
at the edge
of what wraps
you round.

It may take long
and long
for its length
to fall away,
for the words
of this blessing

to unwind
in folds
about your feet.

By then
you will no longer
need them.

By then this blessing
will have pressed itself
into your waking flesh,
will have passed
into your bones,
will have traveled
every vein

until it comes to rest
inside the chambers
of your heart
that beats to
the rhythm
of benediction

and the cadence
of release.

Therefore I Will Hope

Blessings for
Holy Week & Easter

*A very large crowd spread
their cloaks on the road.*
—MATTHEW 21:8

BLESSING OF PALMS
For Palm Sunday

This blessing
can be heard coming
from a long way off.

This blessing
is making
its steady way
up the road
toward you.

This blessing
blooms in the throats
of women,
springs from the hearts
of men,
tumbles out of the mouths
of children.

This blessing
is stitched into
the seams
of the cloaks

that line the road,
etched into
the branches
that trace the path,
echoes in
the breathing
of the willing colt,
the click
of the donkey's hoof
against the stones.

Something is rising
beneath this blessing.
Something will try
to drown it out.

But this blessing
cannot be turned back,
cannot be made
to still its voice,
cannot cease
to sing its praise
of the One who comes
along the way
it makes.

*"Hosanna! Blessed is the one
who comes in the name
of the Lord!"*
—MARK 11:9

BLESSED IS THE ONE
For Palm Sunday

Blessed is the One
who comes to us
by the way of love
poured out with abandon.

Blessed is the One
who walks toward us
by the way of grace
that holds us fast.

Blessed is the One
who calls us to follow
in the way of blessing,
in the path of joy.

BLESSING THAT BECOMES EMPTY AS IT GOES
For Passion Sunday

This blessing
keeps nothing
for itself.
You can find it
by following the path
of what it has let go,
of what it has learned
it can live without.

Say this blessing out loud
a few times
and you will hear
the hollow places
within it,
how it echoes
in a way
that gives your voice
back to you
as if you had never
heard it before.

Yet this blessing
would not be mistaken

for any other,
as if,
in its emptying,
it had lost
what makes it
most itself.

It simply desires
to have room enough
to welcome
what comes.

Today,
it's you.

So come and sit
in this place
made holy
by its hollows.
You think you have
too much to do,
too little time,
too great a weight
of responsibility
that none but you
can carry.

I tell you,
lay it down.
Just for a moment,
if that's what you
can manage at first.

Five minutes.
Lift up your voice—
in laughter,
in weeping,
it does not matter—
and let it ring against
these spacious walls.

Do this
until you can hear
the spaces within
your own breathing.
Do this
until you can feel
the hollow in your heart
where something
is letting go,
where something
is making way.

Mary took a pound of costly perfume
made of pure nard, anointed Jesus' feet,
and wiped them with her hair.
—John 12:3

Blessing for the Anointing

Some with ointment.
Some with tears.
Me, today,
with words
gathered and treasured,
carried and poured out
for you
wherever you are.

May you welcome this
as what it is:
a needful extravagance,
an offering both lavish
and crucial
that has let go
of everything
to lay itself at your feet
and tell you

I see you.
I bless you.

And you,
where can you go
that you do not need
this anointing,
this blessing that drenches
the one who gives,
the one who receives?

*Then he poured water into a basin
and began to wash the disciples' feet
and to wipe them with the towel
that was tied around him.*
—JOHN 13:5

BLESSING YOU CANNOT TURN BACK
For Holy Thursday

As if you could
stop this blessing
from washing
over you.

As if you could
turn it back,
could return it
from your body
to the bowl,
from the bowl
to the pitcher,
from the pitcher
to the hand
that set this blessing
on its way.

As if you could
change the course
by which this blessing
flows.

As if you could
control how it
pours over you—
unbidden,
unsought,
unasked,

yet startling
in the way
it matches the need
you did not know
you had.

As if you could
become undrenched.

As if you could
resist gathering it up
in your two hands
and letting your body
follow the arc
this blessing makes.

> *"This cup is the new covenant in my blood. Do this, as often as you drink it, in remembrance of me."*
> —1 CORINTHIANS 11:25

BLESSING THE BREAD, THE CUP
For Holy Thursday

Let us bless the bread
that gives itself to us
with its terrible weight,
its infinite grace.

Let us bless the cup
poured out for us
with a love
that makes us anew.

Let us gather
around these gifts
simply given
and deeply blessed.

And then let us go
bearing the bread,
carrying the cup,
laying the table
within a hungering world.

They went to a place called Gethsemane;
and he said to his disciples,
"Sit here while I pray."
—MARK 14:32

BLESSING FOR STAYING AWAKE
For Holy Thursday

Even in slumber,
even in dreaming,
even in sorrow,
even in pain:

awake, awake,
awake my soul
to the One who keeps vigil
at all times for you.

Carrying the cross by himself,
he went out to what is called
The Place of the Skull.
—JOHN 19:17

BLESSING THAT MAKES A WAY FOR YOU
For Good Friday

What I know is
that this blessing will begin
as soon as you set out.

That this blessing
will meet you
in every step.

That it is gladly
bound to you
and cannot do
without you.

That you are
part of the path
this blessing makes:
that it creates a way
not only for you
but through you
and in you,
that it finds its road
as you find yours.

I can hardly fathom
how it is
that this blessing
is already waiting for you
even as you fashion it,
step by faltering step.

But there it is,
in all its wending mystery.

So may you meet it
with courage.
May you enter it
with clarity.
May you walk it
with wisdom.
May you travel it
with joy.

May you come to it
not as one buffeted
by chance
but as one
who has chosen.
Uncertain, perhaps;
unready, perhaps;
but this path.
This one.
With abandon.
This.

"They will look on the one
whom they have pierced."
—JOHN 19:37

WHAT ABIDES
For Good Friday

You will know
this blessing
by how it
does not stay still,
by the way it
refuses to rest
in one place.

You will recognize it
by how it takes
first one form,
then another:

now running down
the face of the mother
who watches the breaking
of the child
she had borne,

now in the stance
of the woman
who followed him here

and will not leave him
bereft.

Now it twists in anguish
on the mouth of the friend
whom he loved;

now it bares itself
in the wound,
the cry,
the finishing and
final breath.

This blessing
is not in any one
of these alone.

It is what
binds them
together.

It is what dwells
in the space
between them,
though it be torn
and gaping.

It is what abides
in the tear
the rending makes.

*All his acquaintances, including
the women who had followed him
from Galilee, stood at a distance,
watching these things.*
—LUKE 23:49

STILL
For Good Friday

This day
let all stand still
in silence,
in sorrow.

Sun and moon
be still.

Earth
be still.

Still
the waters.

Still
the wind.

Let the ground
gape in stunned
lamentation.

Let it weep
as it receives
what it thinks
it will not
give up.

Let it groan
as it gathers
the One
who was thought
forever stilled.

Time
be still.

Watch
and wait.

Still.

They took the body of Jesus
and wrapped it with the spices
in linen cloths.
—JOHN 19:40

SONG OF THE WINDING SHEET
For Good Friday

We never
would have wished it
to come to this,
yet we call
these moments holy
as we hold you.

Holy the tending,
holy the winding,
holy the leaving
as in the living.

Holy the silence,
holy the stillness,
holy the turning
and returning to earth.

Blessed is the One
who came
in the name,

blessed is the One
who laid
himself down,

blessed is the One
emptied for us,

blessed is the One
wearing the shroud.

Holy the waiting,
holy the grieving,
holy the shadows
and gathering night.

Holy the darkness,
holy the hours,
holy the hope
turning toward light.

"The LORD is my portion," says my soul,
"therefore I will hope in him."
—LAMENTATIONS 3:24

THEREFORE I WILL HOPE
For Holy Saturday

I have no cause
to linger beside
this place of death,

no reason
to keep vigil
where life has left,

and yet I cannot go,
cannot bring myself
to cleave myself
from here,

can only pray
that this waiting
might yet be a blessing
and this grieving
yet a blessing
and this stone
yet a blessing
and this silence
yet a blessing
still.

*I have become
like a broken vessel.*
—Psalm 31:12

Blessing for a Broken Vessel
For Holy Saturday

Do not despair.
You hold the memory
of what it was
to be whole.

It lives deep
in your bones.
It abides
in your heart
that has been torn
and mended
a hundred times.
It persists
in your lungs
that know the mystery
of what it means
to be full,
to be empty,
to be full again.

I am not asking you
to give up your grip

on the shards you clasp
so close to you

but to wonder
what it would be like
for those jagged edges
to meet each other
in some new pattern
that you have never imagined,
that you have never dared
to dream.

*Mary Magdalene and the
other Mary were there,
sitting opposite the tomb.*
—MATTHEW 27:61

IN THE BREATH, ANOTHER BREATHING
For Holy Saturday

Let it be
that on this day
we will expect
no more of ourselves
than to keep
breathing
with the bewildered
cadence
of lungs that will not
give up the ghost.

Let it be
we will expect
little but
the beating of
our heart,
stubborn in
its repeating rhythm
that will not
cease to sound.

Let it be
we will
still ourselves
enough to hear
what may yet
come to echo:
as if in the breath,
another breathing;
as if in the heartbeat,
another heart.

Let it be
we will not
try to fathom
what comes
to meet us
in the stillness
but simply open
to the approach
of a mystery
we hardly dared
to dream.

Be a rock of refuge for me,
a strong fortress to save me.
—PSALM 31:2

THE ART OF ENDURING
For Holy Saturday

This blessing
can wait as long
as you can.

Longer.

This blessing
began eons ago
and knows the art
of enduring.

This blessing
has passed
through ages
and generations,
witnessed the turning
of centuries,
weathered the spiraling
of history.

This blessing
is in no rush.

This blessing
will plant itself
by your door.

This blessing
will keep vigil
and chant prayers.

This blessing
will bring a friend
for company.

This blessing
will pack a lunch
and a thermos
of coffee.

This blessing
will bide
its sweet time

until it hears
the beginning
of breath,
the stirring
of limbs,
the stretching,
reaching,
rising

of what had lain
dead within you

and is ready
to return.

"He is not here; for he has been raised, as he said."
—Matthew 28:6

Risen
For Easter Day

If you are looking
for a blessing,
do not linger
here.

Here
is only
emptiness,
a hollow,
a husk
where a blessing
used to be.

This blessing
was not content
in its confinement.

It could not abide
its isolation,
the unrelenting silence,
the pressing stench
of death.

So if it is
a blessing
you seek,
open your own
mouth.

Fill your lungs
with the air
this new
morning brings

and then
release it
with a cry.

Hear how the blessing
breaks forth
in your own voice,

how your own lips
form every word
you never dreamed
to say.

See how the blessing
circles back again,
wanting you to
repeat it,
but louder,

how it draws you,
pulls you,

sends you
to proclaim
its only word:

Risen.
Risen.
Risen.

"Woman, why are you weeping?
Whom are you looking for?"
—JOHN 20:15

SEEN
For Easter Day

You had not imagined
that something so empty
could fill you
to overflowing,

and now you carry
the knowledge
like an awful treasure
or like a child
that curls itself
within your heart:

how the emptiness
will bear forth
a new world
you cannot fathom
but on whose edge
you stand.

So why do you linger?
You have seen,
and so you are

154   *Circle of Grace*

already blessed.
You have been seen,
and so you are
the blessing.

There is no other word
you need.
There is simply
to go
and tell.
There is simply
to begin.

The Magdalene's Blessing
For Easter Day

You hardly imagined
standing here,
everything you ever loved
suddenly returned to you,
looking you in the eye
and calling your name.

And now
you do not know
how to abide this hole
in the center
of your chest,
where a door
slams shut
and swings open
at the same time,
turning on the hinge
of your aching
and hopeful heart.

I tell you,
this is not a banishment
from the garden.

This is an invitation,
a choice,
a threshold,
a gate.

This is your life
calling to you
from a place
you could never
have dreamed,
but now that you
have glimpsed its edge,
you cannot imagine
choosing any other way.

So let the tears come
as anointing,
as consecration,
and then
let them go.

Let this blessing
gather itself around you.

Let it give you
what you will need
for this journey.

You will not remember
the words—
they do not matter.

All you need to remember
is how it sounded
when you stood
in the place of death
and heard the living
call your name.

When We Breathe Together

Together

Blessings for
Ascension & Pentecost

*"Stay here in the city
until you have been clothed
with power from on high."*
—LUKE 24:49

STAY

I know how your mind
rushes ahead,
trying to fathom
what could follow this.
What will you do,
where will you go,
how will you live?

You will want
to outrun the grief.
You will want
to keep turning toward
the horizon,
watching for what was lost
to come back,
to return to you
and never leave again.

For now,
hear me when I say
all you need to do
is to still yourself,

is to turn toward one another,
is to stay.

Wait
and see what comes
to fill
the gaping hole
in your chest.
Wait with your hands open
to receive what could never come
except to what is empty
and hollow.

You cannot know it now,
cannot even imagine
what lies ahead,
but I tell you
the day is coming
when breath will
fill your lungs
as it never has before,
and with your own ears
you will hear words
coming to you new
and startling.
You will dream dreams
and you will see the world
ablaze with blessing.

Wait for it.
Still yourself.
Stay.

*While he was blessing them,
he withdrew from them and
was carried up into heaven.*
—Luke 24:51

Blessing the Distance

It is a mystery to me
how as the distance
between us grows,
the larger this blessing
becomes,

as if the shape of it
depends on absence,
as if it finds its form
not by what
it can cling to
but by the space
that arcs
between us.

As this blessing
makes its way,
first it will cease
to measure itself
by time.

Then it will release
how attached it has become

to this place
where we have lived,
where we have learned
to know one another
in proximity and
presence.

Next this blessing
will abandon
the patterns
in which it moved,
the habits that helped it
recognize itself,
the familiar pathways
it traced.

Finally this blessing
will touch its fingers
to your brow,
your eyes,
your mouth;
it will hold
your beloved face
in both its hands,

and then
it will let you go;
it will loose you
into your life;
it will leave
each hindering thing

until all that breathes
between us
is blessing
and all that beats
between us
is grace.

*They worshiped him, and returned
to Jerusalem with great joy.*
—LUKE 24:52

IN THE LEAVING

In the leaving,
in the letting go,
let there be this
to hold onto
at the last:

the enduring of love,
the persisting of hope,
the remembering of joy,

the offering of gratitude,
the receiving of grace,
the blessing of peace.

When the day of Pentecost had come,
they were all together in one place.
—ACTS 2:1

WHEN WE BREATHE TOGETHER

This is the blessing
we cannot speak
by ourselves.

This is the blessing
we cannot summon
by our own devices,
cannot shape
to our own purposes,
cannot bend
to our own will.

This is the blessing
that comes
when we leave behind
our aloneness,
when we gather
together,
when we turn
toward one another.

This is the blessing
that blazes among us

when we speak
the words
strange to our ears,

when we finally listen
into the chaos,

when we breathe together
at last.

Divided tongues, as of fire,
appeared among them, and a
tongue rested on each of them.
—ACTS 2:3

THIS GRACE THAT SCORCHES US

Here's one thing
you must understand
about this blessing:
it is not
for you alone.

It is stubborn
about this.
Do not even try
to lay hold of it
if you are by yourself,
thinking you can carry it
on your own.

To bear this blessing,
you must first take yourself
to a place where everyone
does not look like you
or think like you,
a place where they do not
believe precisely as you believe,
where their thoughts
and ideas and gestures

are not exact echoes
of your own.

Bring your sorrow.
Bring your grief.
Bring your fear.
Bring your weariness,
your pain,
your disgust at how broken
the world is,
how fractured,
how fragmented
by its fighting,
its wars,
its hungers,
its penchant for power,
its ceaseless repetition
of the history it refuses
to rise above.

I will not tell you
this blessing will fix all that.

But in the place
where you have gathered,
wait.
Watch.
Listen.
Lay aside your inability
to be surprised,
your resistance to what you
do not understand.

See then whether this blessing
turns to flame on your tongue,
sets you to speaking
what you cannot fathom

or opens your ear
to a language
beyond your imagining
that comes as a knowing
in your bones,
a clarity
in your heart
that tells you

this is the reason
we were made:
for this ache
that finally opens us,

for this struggle,
this grace
that scorches us
toward one another
and into
the blazing day.

*All of them were filled with
the Holy Spirit and began
to speak in other languages.*
—ACTS 2:4

BLESSING THAT UNDOES US

On the day
you are wearing
your certainty
like a cloak
and your sureness
goes before you
like a shield
or like a sword,

may the sound
of God's name
spill from your lips
as you have never
heard it before.

May your knowing
be undone.
May mystery
confound your
understanding.

May the Divine
rain down

in strange syllables
yet with
an ancient familiarity,
a knowing borne
in the blood,
the ear,
the tongue,
bringing the clarity
that comes
not in stone
or in steel
but in fire,
in flame.

May there come
one searing word—
enough to bare you
to the bone,
enough to set
your heart ablaze,
enough to make you
whole again.

Each one heard them speaking
in the native language of each.
—ACTS 2:6

WHAT THE FIRE GIVES

You had thought that fire
only consumed,
only devoured,
only took for itself,
leaving merely ash
and memory
of something
you had believed,
if not permanent,
would be long enough,
enduring enough,
to be nearly
eternal.

So when you felt
the scorching on your lips,
the searing in your heart,
you could not
at first believe
that flame could be
so generous,
that when it came to you—
you, in your sackcloth

and sorrow—
it did not come
to consume,
to take still more
than everything.

What surprised you most
were not the syllables
that spilled from
your scalded,
astonished mouth—
though that was miracle
enough,
to have words
burn through
what had been numb,
to find your tongue
aflame with a language
you did not know
you knew—

no, what came
as greatest gift
was to be so heard
in the place
of your deepest
silence,
to be so seen
within the blazing,
to be met
with such completeness
by what the fire gives.

WHERE THE HANDS MEET

———————

*A Blessing to Begin
Ordinary Time*

"The whole earth is full of his glory."
—Isaiah 6:3

Blessing the Ordinary

Let these words
lay themselves
like a blessing
upon your head,
your shoulders,

as if,
like hands,
they could pass on
to you
what you most need
for this day,

as if they could
anoint you
not merely for
the path ahead

but for this
ordinary moment
that opens itself
to you—

opens itself
like another hand
that unfurls itself,
that reaches out
to gather
these words
in the bowl
of its palm.

You may think
this blessing
lives within
these words,

but I tell you
it lives
in the opening
and in the reaching;

it lives
in the ache
where this blessing
begins;

it lives
in the hollow
made by the place
where the hands
of this blessing
meet.

About the Author

Jan Richardson is a writer, artist, and ordained minister in the United Methodist Church. She serves as director of The Wellspring Studio, LLC, and makes her home in Florida.

You can find her distinctive artwork, writing, and more at her blogs and websites:

The Painted Prayerbook
paintedprayerbook.com

The Advent Door
adventdoor.com

Jan Richardson Images
janrichardsonimages.com

and

janrichardson.com

Made in the USA
Monee, IL
16 September 2023

42861369R10106